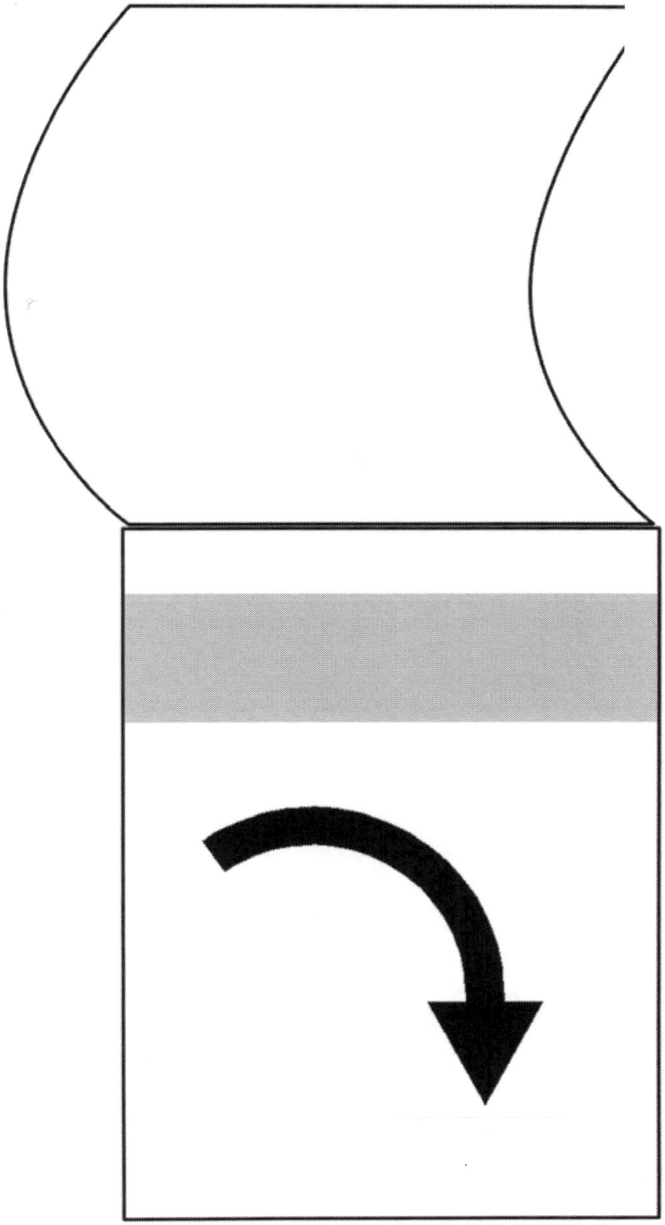

THE SPRY GUIDE TO
CREATING A WEBSITE

COPYRIGHT 2010 TO SPRYGUIDES.CO.UK
ISBN: 978-1-4461-3622-5
FIRST EDITION

AUTHORS EMAIL: CARL.MASON@SPRYGUIDES.CO.UK
FIND MORE SPRY GUIDES AT WWW.SPRYGUIDES.CO.UK

Contents...

- 1   You Will Need
- 2   A Good Reason
- 3   About You
- 4   Computers & The Internet
- 6   Code Editing Software
- 7   Image Editing Software
- 8   The Golden Rules
- 9   Finding Inspiration
- 10 Colour Schemes
- 11 Fonts
- 12 Making a Template
- 15 Web Hosting
- 19 Domain Names
- 20 File Uploading
- 24 The Results
- 26 What Next
- 27 Trouble Shooter
- 28 Glossary
- 32 About The Author
- 33 Further Reading

About This Book

This book is intended to be your pocket guide to getting a website online. While it doesn't teach you the in's and out's of HTML or the other coding languages you may need, it does explore the types of software and the configuration of your site. Think of it as your tick-book and notepad - ensuring you create your site correctly.

You Will Need...

With the right resources, making a website can be a very straight-forward process. The list below shows some of the main things you will need to make your website. You can tick off each item as you acquire it...

- [x] A Good Reason
- [ ] Code Editing Software
- [ ] Image Editing Software
- [ ] A Good Design
- [ ] Web Hosting
- [ ] Domain Name
- [ ] Reliable Internet Connection
- [ ] A Basic Computer
- [ ] File Uploading Software
- [ ] Internet Explorer
- [ ] Firefox
- [ ] Email Address

How Much Money?

You don't need a massive budget to make a good website. If you can spare the patience and time you can create a fantastic website from as little as £20 - it's true, I've done it many times!

The mandatory costs for a website are the web-address (less than £10) and the hosting (from about £2.00 per month) - although with a little compromise you can even get these for free.

If you truly want to save money, you are going to need to learn some computer skills. At the very least HTML and ideally PHP (both geeky sounding words - and they are).

If you have the money available, you can hire someone else to take care of the tricky bits for you.

Don't give up if there is already a website which will be similar to the type you want to create.

Everything can be improved so take this opportunity to see how they are doing things and what could be improved - then build a better website!

Plus - you can see where that site is advertising and copy the demographic!

A Good Reason...

The internet is a very saturated place, overflowing with websites about everything from the latest celebrity gossip, to funny videos and serious medical discoveries. Just about anything is acceptable (within the law, of course) and everything will have an audience of some shape or size.

So where will your website sit in the jungle of internet sites? Here are some questions to help you decide...

What Is Your Website About?

Why Will People Want To Visit Your Site?

What Other Sites Are You Competing With?

Chances are you will have ticked just a few 'good' boxes but don't worry - it's unlikely anyone will tick more than five.

However, if you have ticked any 'Need to Learn' boxes you really should make an effort to learn these skills - they will make a massive difference to your website.

Each skills listed can be learnt - often for free!

About You (Part 1)...

Great, now you have a rough idea of why people will be using your website and where it will sit in the online world. Before we go any further, take a second to think about how much effort you want to spend on your site.

How many hours per day can you spend working on your site?

How much money, if any, would you like to make from your site?

How much can you afford to spend on creating your website?

How much can you afford to spend on maintaining your website?

Okay, so far we have a rough idea of what you want the site to be and what you are prepared to commit to it. Now we should look at what skills you have that are relevant to creating a website. Tick the box most applicable to you...

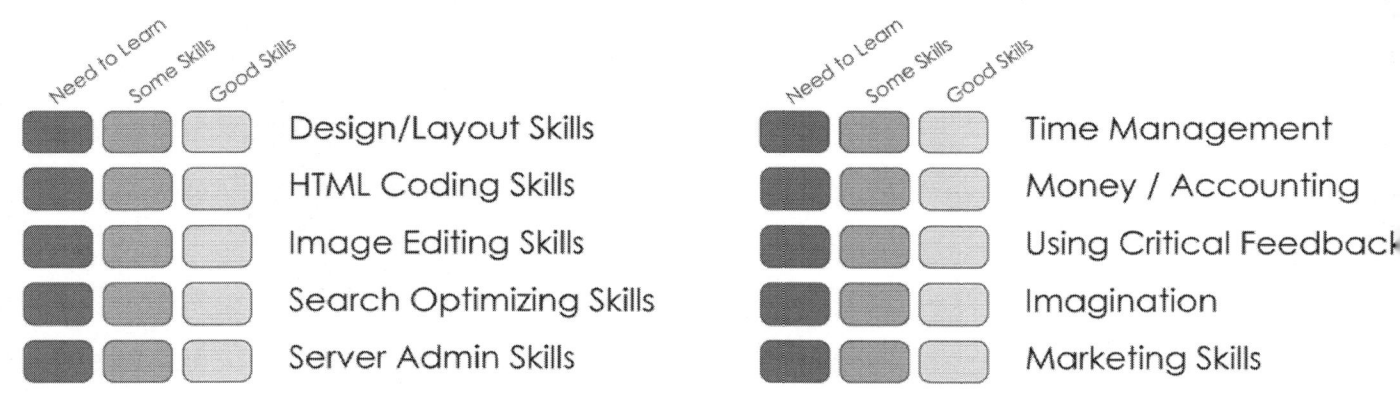

Need to Learn	Some Skills	Good Skills		Need to Learn	Some Skills	Good Skills	
☐	☐	☐	Design/Layout Skills	☐	☐	☐	Time Management
☐	☐	☐	HTML Coding Skills	☐	☐	☐	Money / Accounting
☐	☐	☐	Image Editing Skills	☐	☐	☐	Using Critical Feedback
☐	☐	☐	Search Optimizing Skills	☐	☐	☐	Imagination
☐	☐	☐	Server Admin Skills	☐	☐	☐	Marketing Skills

Try places like Amazon or Ebay for second-hand books - they often have some great quality books available which you can use and scribble in - and often at reduced prices!

Alternatively, your local library should also stock a small selection of books on each of the subjects listed on the previous page!

About You (Part 2)...

Don't worry if you haven't ticked many 'good' boxes on the previous page. The imporant thing is for you to realise where you need to either improve your skills or hire someone else to give you a hand.

In regards to learning new skills - don't be afraid of picking up a book and giving it a good go. Many people tend to flick through a book and are put off by a lot of odd code and geeky language they don't understand. However, the good books will explain how everything works and will walk you through it all.

On the other hand, there are also a lot of free tutorials available on the internet. However, most of these tutorials are written by the average John Smith and may be lacking some of the more professional direction you would get in a book.

Now, based on the tick list on the previous page, list the skills you need to learn and mark them off once you have learnt them...

- [ ]
- [ ]
- [ ]
- [ ]
- [ ]
- [ ]
- [ ]

When looking at internet providers (ISPs) remember to check for Data Caps - these limit the amount of data you can download. If possible find an unlimited supplier.

You should also check that the upload speed is above 500Kbs - any slower and it may take a long time to upload any changes to your website.

Computers & Internet...

On the first page I listed a load of things you will need to create a good website. Before I move onto the more complicated things, like code editors, I wanted to quickly explain why I listed a 'Decent Computer' and 'Reliable Internet' - two seemingly obvious things.

A Decent Computer

The power of your computer decides how many things you can do - and possibly what programs you can run.

I managed to create several decent websites on a 10-year old computer - although it was very frustrating and eventually I bought a new one.

The main downside to a low-power computer is the amount of time you will spend waiting, especially when editing images.

But, if a "fancy pants" computer isn't within your budget just yet you can make-do with what you have - just be prepared for alot of waiting around (use the time to make a cuppa!)

Reliable Internet Connection

Never under-estimate the importance of your internet connection - without it, you might as well not bother making a website.

Believe me, you will be constantly making tweaks and changes - adding new content and finding spelling mistakes forever. Plus, if you running an online shop you will effectively out of business while your internet is down.

My advice, choose a decent broadband supplier with uncapped downloads. If working from home, a normal broadband connection from the likes of Virgin Media will be ideal.

> I always keep a mobile dongle on-hand just incase. Its a great backup should there be a problem with the internet or phone line.

What features would you need in a Code Editor?

If you only planning to make a very basic website it would be pointless to buy software. Alternatively, if you plan to start a business which requires regular designing it may be worth looking into commercial solutions.

Code Editing Software...

We should now start looking at Code Editing Software. This is the program you will use to actually create your website.

Adobe Dreamweaver

Dreamweaver is the long-standing editor of choice. It has been developed over many years and is the favourite of web designers around the world. I find Dreamweaver one of the easiest programs to use as it has alot of build-it functions which make web-design much easier.

However, it comes with a heavy price tag. The latest version currently costs £419 - although you may be able to find used or older versions for a more reasonable price.

I currently use 'CS3' (the lastest is CS5) and I find it to be perfectly suitable. It has built-in uploading, spell checking and is ideal if you like to use more complex feautres like layers. It also supports many different coding languages such PHP and JavaScript.

Kompozer

If you don't fancy paying hundreds of pounds for a code editing program, you might want to try Kompozer. It is a FREE program packed with lots of useful features and an upload facility built-in for saving your website to the internet instantly. During my research I found an huge number of great reviews for Kompozer which indicates it may be a good contender to DreamWeaver.

Download Kompozer From: www.kompozer.net/

!

Even the most basic websites need to look good. A bad look will easily degrade the content of your website - even if the content is just text.

A good looking site will produce more credibility to the work you are publishing.

Image Editing Software...

Hopefully you now have the Code Editor of your choice. Next we should look at your Image Editing Program...

Adobe Photoshop

Photoshop is from the same family as Dreamweaver and is often sold as part of a set. It is the recognised industry favourite for all types of design and image editing.

There have been many versions of Photoshop each with more features than the last. The latest full version retails at around £1000. However, you can find many older versions floating around on eBay for much less.

GIMP

Luckily there is also a free piece of software you can use for image editing. GIMP is an 'open source' program which is freely available to download and use.

Although personally I found it to be a little confusing to use, it may be worth the struggle if it saves alot of money. There is also a fair number of tutorials and books available if you need them.

Download GIMP From: www.gimp.org

Macromedia Fireworks

Fireworks was designed for making websites although it is a few years out of date now. However, I still use a copy from 2001 and I find it very easy to use and the effects are suitable for most sites.

Adobe still maintain this software although they prefer to push Photoshop. The latest version currently retails for around £280. Shopping around for used versions will save you alot of money here.

! No matter what part of your site you are working on you should always think about who is going to be using your site and what they want.

The Golden Rules...

The design of your site is critical to your success. Not only does your site need to look good, it needs to be easy to use. You are also legally required to make it accessible for people with special needs (ie. having a text-only option).

The one rule I've always found helpful is 'Always Kiss' which stands for...

ALWAYS Keep It Simple, Stupid

While slightly degrading, I've sometimes found myself remembering it and having to strip out alot of the design work I've just done because it was simply too much.

Try writing 'Always Kiss' on a sticky note and stick it to your monitor. You'll always remember to keep your design simple and you might even get a quick kiss from your other half (or if your single, a few odd looks and a conversation starter...).

When designing always ask yourself the following questions...

- [ ] Will the user find this useful?
- [ ] Will it load quickly?
- [ ] It is easy to navigate to and from?
- [ ] Is the design consistent?
- [ ] How can it be adapted for users with special needs?
- [ ] Will it look good on a small/big screen?

If you having trouble finding inspiration for a good design you can try making a very simple site first and then build upon that until you have created something you are happy with!

Finding Inspiration...

Designing is all about creating a layout that is right for your visitors. We all like to take credit for a fantastic design but you are allowed to take a few shortcuts. As one of my tutors always said 'Why Re-Invent the Wheel?'

It is perfectly acceptable to look at template sites such as TemplateMonster.com for inspiration and good ideas. Naturally, just remember not to copy what you see. You could, for example, see a colour scheme or menu layout you like. It's not cheating, it's being smart!

Or, if you don't like the idea of using a template site, there are lots of books available specifically to give inspiration. I have a book by Patrick McNeil called 'The Web Designer's Idea Book'. It's full of great examples and is grouped by color, layout, category ect.

If you need some inspiration, try looking at these sites...

- www.TemplateMonster.com
- www.Webdesign-Inspiration.com
- www.DesignFridge.co.uk
- www.WebCreme.com
- www.asiteaday.org

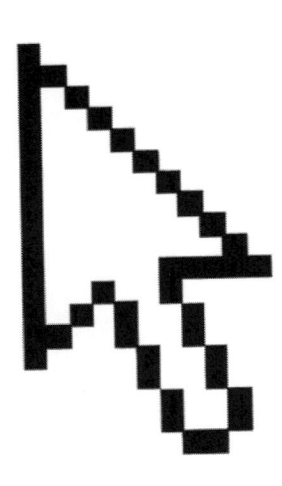

Some colours carry certain 'feelings'. For example, Blue is often seen as a confident and safe colour - which is why it is frequently used by corporations.

If you are going to be creating a very colourful site you might find it worthwhile buying a book about the effects of colours.

Colour Scheme...

The colour scheme you pick can make or break your website. You need to consider the type of people that will be using your site and what they will expect to see. A good place to start is by looking at any material you already have. For example, do you have a logo or some stationary which has colours you could transfer to your site?

Just to make sure you have the perfect colour scheme, here are a few little rules to remember (as always, rules can be bent if you think the scheme works well!).

- [ ] Is the text easy to read on the background
- [ ] Do your colours look natural together? Check a colour wheel if your not sure.
- [ ] Will any colours be overwhelming compared to the others?
- [ ] Ask yourself 'why' you have chosen that colour
- [ ] Have you remembered white? It can be a very clean and modern colour!

If your happy with your colour scheme you can make a note of it below...

You can find a great collection of colour schemes at:

www.colorcombos.com

You can use unusual fonts for headers by creating small images with text.

Although this will make your site load slower and become less 'Search Engine' friendly - it could make it look nicer.

Fonts...

The next thing to look at is the font you use on your website. You must ensure your font is easy to read and suitable for your target audience. Below is a table of common and safe fonts you can use...

Arial — Arial is the standard 'modern' font. It has a very clear style and reads very easy. However, it doesn't work that well when the size is reduced. ☐

Verdana — Verdana is made to look good at small sizes. I use this font on most of my sites and for any footers. ☐

Courier — This font is ideal for long pages of text as it is has set gaps between the letters. ☐

Tahoma — Another easy to read modern font. This font is good for long pages of text if you want a more modern feel. ☐

Times New — Times New Roman is favoured by older-readers. This font has the feel of a newspaper and academic material. ☐

A word of warning: Not every font on your computer will be available on another persons. If the font you have selected isn't available the readers computer will decide which one to use - which may not look as good as the font you chose. For a complete list of compatible fonts check: www.ampsoft.net/webdesign-l/WindowsMacFonts.html

If you already know CSS or JavaScript you can create a feature which will allow visitors to increase (or decrease) the size of text on your website to suit their vision or preferences.

Fonts...

Does Size Matter? It's what you do with it that counts. But when it comes to your websites font you need to make sure it is suitable for your readers. For example, it needs to be large enough to read without taking too much space. Generally, size 12 is a good size to use. Size 10 is about the smallest you should go for most fonts with size 14 to 16 as a large font.

Many larger websites have an added function where the reader is able to enlarge the font to make it readable. It should be noted that you are legally obliged to make your site accessible for users with special needs. Plus, the next time I lose my glasses, I will still be able to use your site!

If you want to use a special font on your website there are two methods you can use. First, you can write the text as part of an image. While this allows you to display a nice header it isn't suitable for an entire page of text and is a real pain to update.

The alternative method is to use a technique called 'Dynamic Text Replacement'. You will need a decent level of HTML and PHP knowledge to make sense of it though. If you would like to use the technique, visit: http://artypapers.com/csshelppile/pcdtr/

?

If there is anything you feel you could improve, now is the best time.

If you make a site and then learn a new skill you will often find yourself changing most of the work you have previously completed.

Lets Recap...

Time for a quick recap.

So far we have looked at quite a few things and you should of had a fair list of things you needed to work on. Here is a quick list of everything you should have learnt and done...

- ☐ Decided the purpose of your site
- ☐ Installed a Code Editor
- ☐ Installed an Image Editor
- ☐ Decided on a Colour Scheme
- ☐ Found some inspiration
- ☐ Found a good Font
- ☐ Made a List of Skills to Learn
- ☐ Learnt the skills on your list

So far so good. If you haven't already done so, it may be worth investing in some good books about HTML, PHP and the Code/Image Editors you are using - or, alternatively, find some good tutorials online.

Through the next few pages I will start walking you through creating your template. It is therefore important you are reasonably happy with your skills. Try going back to the skills checklist to make sure there's nothing you need to work on.

Don't forget there are many professionals who would be more than happy to help you out.

Try **www.NovusDesigns.co.uk**. Okay, I admit it, that was just a shameless plug for my company - but we'd be happy to work with you.

Another source of free help can be found on Internet Forums.

If using a Search Engine, try searching for your problem with the word 'Forum' on the end. You can post your problem for others to help you with - and maybe even help someone else too!

! I always find it useful to start with a simple template and build-up slowly until I have create a unique and interesting design.

Templates...

Templates are an easy way of making your website. The idea is that you make one page with no content (just the logo and menu ect...). You can then just make a copy and add your content. In this section I will guide you through making a simple table-based template. You can experiment and edit as much as you like.

Before we start, I must stress again that this book does not teach you how to use your editing program or more HTML than has already been covered. It is possible to make a template without learning HTML but it always helps if you do.

Our Aim
The aim of this template is to create a very simple, but usable, outline for a demo site. You can use this technique to make your own website

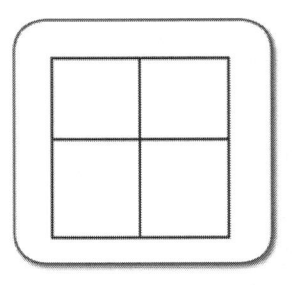

Start by making a table with 2 columns and 2 rows. We will use the top-left box for you logo, the bottom-left for your menu, the bottom-right for your content and the top-right will be left empty.

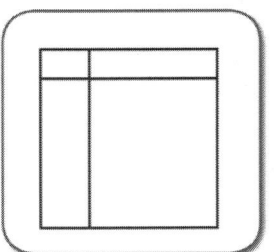

Set the top-left column to be 200 pixels wide and 150 pixels high. You can change the size to suit your logo but leave plenty of space around the edge of the logo (at least 10 pixels).

!

You can play around with the layout of your website.

Your visitors will expect to find the menu on the left hand-side or at the top of your screen so if you move it - make it obvious!

Templates...

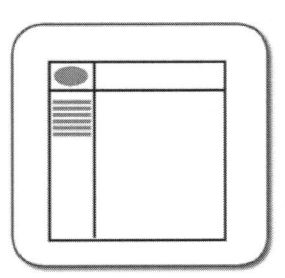

Insert your logo into the top-left box and type your menu into the bottom-left box. You should now have something that looks like the image on the left.

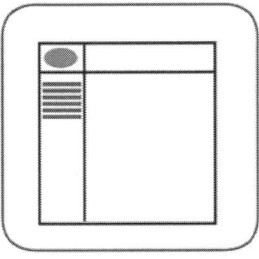

Highlight the first menu link and add a hyperlink to that page. You will need to check the instructions for the code editor you are using but remember to add the file extention (this is usually '.html', '.php' or something similar. Repeat this for each link.

If you like, you can remove the borders and add a background too.

You can now add the content to your new page. The next time you want to create a page simply open the template file and the save it under a different name.

Congratulations - you've just finished your template. You can now use this template to create a website. Naturally as your skills improve you will want to make fancier layouts and add extra effects but the template above is a very common starting point.

!

Search engines (like Google) will take the name of the page into account when indexing your website.

Therefore, try to ensure your page names relate to the content.

A Few Small Points...

Use the template you have just made to create your website. It may not look amazing yet but the template is just the shell - it's what you put inside that will make it great.

One thing I should point out is that your homepage must be called 'index'. This is because when someone accesses your website the server will look for the index file first. If the server can't find an index file, it will just show a list of all the files - which isn't very inviting for your visitors.

It often helps to name files after what they are about. For example, call your about page... 'about'. You can't use spaces, captial letters or symbols in your file name though!

How To Get Online...

Now that you have a site prepared, we should talk about how to get it online. You will need the following:-

- ☐ Web Hosting
- ☐ Domain Name
- ☐ File Uploading Software

All of these things are relatively cheap to obtain. The next few pages will discuss both in detail.

!

If you are going to create a website with lots of videos or music - look for a specialist hosting service as these will use a significant amount of valuable bandwidth.

Web Hosting...

Web hosting is the term given to saving your website to a special computer, also known as a server. Web Servers are constantly connected to the internet and have the sole purpose of allowing the world to access and download your website.

There are literally thousands of hosting companies with various different products and prices. Take a look through the following and tick the boxes which apply to you...

☐ Shared Hosting - This option is best for small sites and is cheaper

☐ Dedicated Hosting - The option is best for busy sites and is expensive

Hosting companies offer an arsenal of features. However, for a simple site you ony need to worry about two things; Storage and Bandwidth.

Storage is the amount of space on the server. I usually offer 100MB with sites I host which serves the vast majority of people. If you want to have videos, music or lots of photos you will need considerably more.

Bandwidth is the amount of data you can transfer from the server to your visitors computer. This is often measured in gigabytes (GB). One gigabyte is enough for about 10,000 page views. Again, video and music will need far more bandwidth.

> When looking to a hosting company make sure you find a reliable and recommended provider. If your hosting fails your website will be offline until they fix it. We recommend:
>
> **www.NovusHosting.co.uk**
> (Yeah, another shameless plug!)

! Try to pick a memorable domain. Either an unusual combination (eg. del.icio.us) or a description of your company.

Domain Name...

Your domain name is the website address you type into your browser to view a website (for example: www.NovusDesigns.co.uk).

Domain names have to be registered through registrars and they will always incur a cost. Luckily, domains start from as little as £10.00. The only restriction on your domain name is whether anyone else has already registered it.

The suffix at the end of your domain is called a TLD (Top Level Domain) and is available in whole host of different choices. Some of the more common ones are:-

☐	.com	☐	.org	☐	.be	☐	.in	☐	.org.uk
☐	.co.uk	☐	.info	☐	.tel	☐	.im	☐	.eu
☐	.net	☐	.me	☐	.me.uk	☐	.tv	☐	.mobi

There are plenty of other endings available. Most countries have their own TLDs and some, included above, form useful words. For example, Montenegro's TLD is '.me' which can be used to make memorable web addresses.

A new domain '.co' is also about to become publically available (from the end of July 2010).

So, what you need to do now is think about what domain you would like. The best way to check if a domain has already been registered or not is to simply type it into your browser. If a website isn't found there is a good chance the domain is available. You can write the domain you want in the box below if it helps remember it.

[   ] . [   ]

> **!**
>
> If you are going to register lots of domains it may be cheaper to setup a reseller account with a registrar. These will usually give you the option of setting the price of each type of domain.
>
> If you set the price low and buy from yourself you could save as much as 50%!

Domain Name...

Registering your domain name is fairly straight-forward. First you need to find a registrar. There are load of registrars on the internet and they all charge different amounts for domains.

Personally, I've always used 123-reg.co.uk but GoDaddy.co.uk is also very popular. Both offer a fantastic service with very reasonable prices - plus, they also offer additional services like email and hosting if you need it.

Here are some quick rules when it comes to registering your domain name...

- [ ] Shop around to find the best price
- [ ] Many hosting providers offer a free domain name
- [ ] Choose a memorable domain that describes your business
- [ ] If your chosen domain is taken, try a different TLD (eg .co.uk instead of .com)
- [ ] You must enter truthful contact details with your domain
- [ ] Only with .co.uk domain you can 'hide' your contact details
- [ ] You can see who owns a domain by performing a 'whois' search
- [ ] You must renew your domain regularly, or register it for several years
- [ ] Domains take upto 24 hours to register and update - plan for this time

Because of the amount of time it takes for domain names to update, it may be worth registering your domain before you go looking for a hosting company

!

Remeber to register different versions of your domain.

For example, if you have bought the '.com' version, try buying '.co.uk' and '.net'.

Domain Setup...

Before I go into the relatively easy way of setting up your domain, I should first tell you about how the internet works.

Every computer that connects to the internet (servers included) is assigned a unique number - known as an IP. When you type in a web address your computer has find a local 'internet address book' which tells your computer what IP the web address should connect to. These 'address books' are called Nameservers.

Your shiny new web address is currently not linked to any nameservers so whenever someone types in it - it won't go anywhere. So you will need to tell your domain registrar your nameservers.

If you don't know what your nameservers are, contact your hosting provider - each provider has their own set of nameservers. Usually, a nameserver is something like: ns1.novushosting.co.uk.

You always need to have at least two nameservers - just incase one stops working. Your domain registrar will have an area on their website where you can update your nameservers. It might be helpful to write your name servers below...

☐ Tick this box when you have updated your nameservers

Remember, it can take upto 24 hours for your domain to be updated worldwide.

For any advanced domain features you may need to learn how to use DNS.

Don't worry, it's fairly simple!

Domain Name...

One last note about domain names.

If the domain you have chosen has already be registered by someone else it may be worth checking if it's available for sale.

Unfortunately it has become very common for people to register domains purely to sell them on for a higher price - sometimes for hundreds of pounds or more. There are some popular sites worth checking.

- Sedo.co.uk
- SellDomain.info
- DomainMonster.com
- ImpressiveDomains.com

It may also be worth checking regular auction sites such as eBay and GumTree, a few people sell domains on these sites as well.

Anything you upload may count towards you Bandwidth limit - check with your hosting provider!

File Uploading...

The term 'File Uploading' refers to the process of copying your website files from your computer to your hosting servers. Most hosting providers offer a browser based system to help you do this but they tend to be very slow and cope badly with large numbers of files.

The better way of uploading your files is by FTP (which stands for File Transfer Protocol - don't worry, it just one of those complicated sounding words computer geeks love to use).

It is likely you will need to setup an FTP account on your hosting server. The process for doing this varies between providers so you will need to check with your provider for details.

Next, you will need to download some FTP software. All it does it copy your files from computer to host. I recommend a program called 'FileZilla' - a small but very complete program which is available for free.

Download FileZilla From: Filezilla-Project.org

You will need to setup FileZilla (or your chosen FTP program) to connect to your account. To do this you will need...

- ☐ FTP Host (eg. ftp.novusdesigns.co.uk)
- ☐ FTP Username
- ☐ FTP Password
- ☐ Port Number (not always required)

> The settings for FTP vary greatly between different hosting providers. It might be worth checking if your provider has a 'how to guide'.
>
> Don't worry if you get the information wrong - it won't break anything!

> **!** On most hosting servers you have to place files in a certain folder (usally 'www' or 'html').
>
> You can also place sensitive files outside of these folders to prevent anyone from directly viewing them (eg. Password files).

File Uploading...

Once you have setup your FTP software you should start uploading all the files you have created. Some hosting providers require you to upload files to certain folders called 'www' or 'html_public' - you will need to check with your hosting provider for specific details but they normally make it very obvious if you need to.

Uploading your website should be fairly straight forward. If your having problems, check the following...

- [ ] FTP Host is correct
- [ ] FTP Username is correct
- [ ] FTP Password is correct (may be case sensitive)
- [ ] Port Number (not always required) is correct
- [ ] You have not exceeded your quota for uploading
- [ ] Are there any error messages? Try searching online for resolutions
- [ ] Can you login to your hosting account?
- [ ] Are you uploading files into the right folder (usually 'www' or 'public')?

If you still need help try contacting your hosting provider or checking if they have a public forum. FTP is one of those areas where lots of people struggle because of the numerous settings you need to have perfect - chances are other users of your hosting provider have had the same problems.

Does It Work?...

Okay, so you have made a simple website, registered a domain and bought yourself some hosting - and put your website online. The only thing you can do now is test it.

If you have waited for at least 24 hours since updating your domain name you can confidently type it into your browser. Go on try it...

...hopefully, your coming back to this guide with a happy face. If not, check back through the book and make sure you have completed each stage correctly. There is also a trouble-shooter at the end of this section if you need more help.

On the other hand, if you can see your site and can move between pages - congratulations.

Now you need to test your site to make sure it works on all computers across the world. Don't worry, it's fairly easy. Simply view your site using Internet Explorer and then with Mozilla Firefox (an alternative to Internet Explorer). If your site looks fine in both then your all good.

However, chances are there will be something different. This is because Internet Explorer plays to a different rule book than the other major browsers and often requires a bit of extra work to sort out.

Unfortunetly, such things are slightly outside of the scope of this book but you should be able to find a solution by searching the internet or buying any good book on HTML.

If the site is working, check the next page for some good ideas on where to go next...

What Next...

Now that you have a basic working site you need to keep updating it with new content and, if you want, new features.

The best sites are always evolving, improving upon the service it already provides. There are numerous things you can do to change your site but always ask yourself one question...

How Will This Help My Visitors?

When I made my first website it took months and, in all honesty, looked hideous. I tried to make it an 'all-in-one' site including everything I could think of. If there is one piece of advice I can give to anyone, its focus on one or two things - and do it well.

I've made a list of some popular ways of improving your website. All are free to use and are fairly easy to add if you feel like playing around.

- [ ] Add a Forum for your visitors to talk to each other
- [ ] Add a contact form for your visitors to talk to you - or a guest book
- [ ] Learn a more advanced coding language and make your own features
- [ ] Add a 'members only' area
- [ ] Update your design
- [ ] Add an area for mobile devices (like the iPhone)

Site Hit the Fan?...

If your site isn't working don't worry. Chances are there is something simple that has been overlooked. Try using the trouble shooter below...

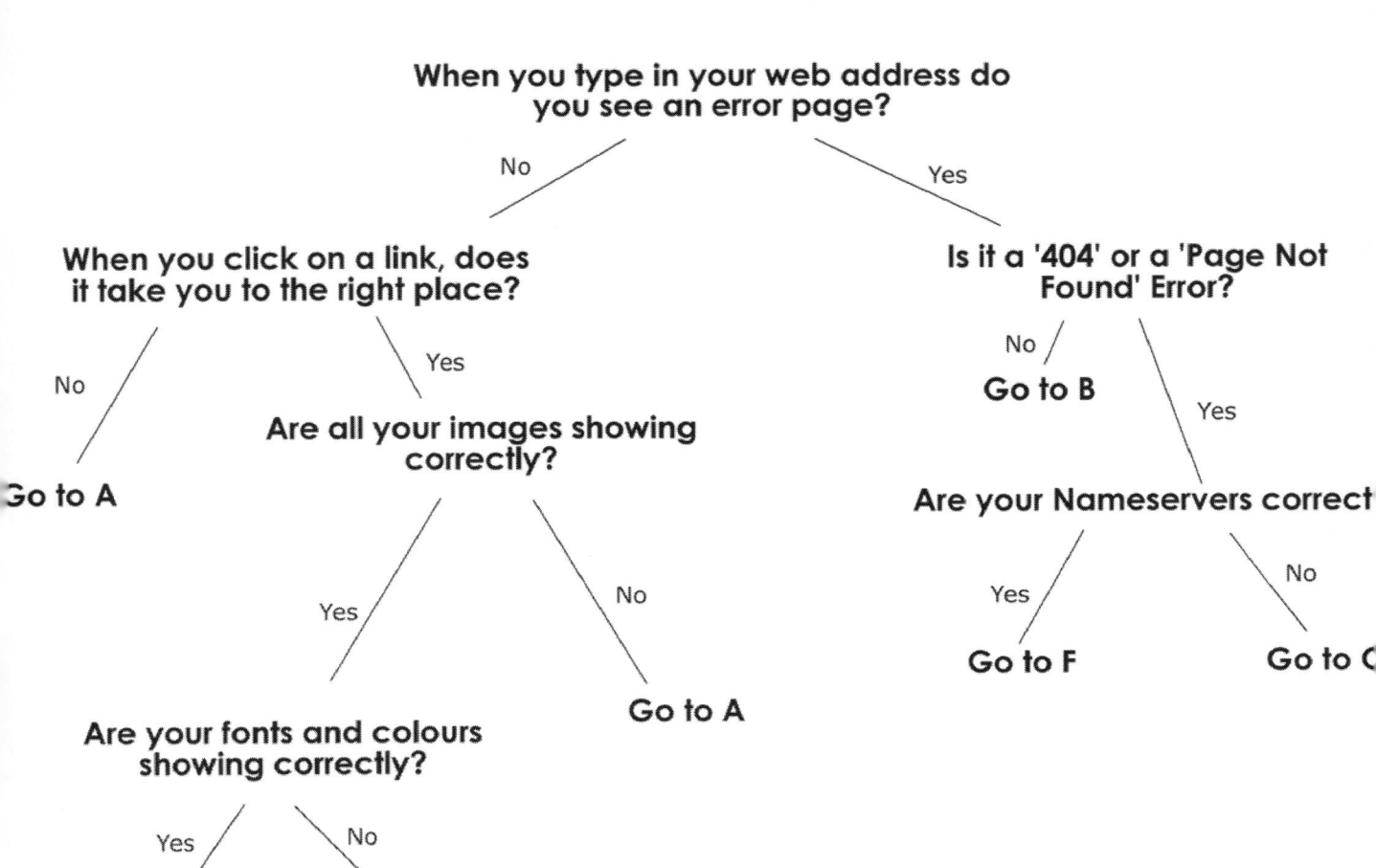

When you type in your web address do you see an error page?

- No → **When you click on a link, does it take you to the right place?**
  - No → Go to A
  - Yes → **Are all your images showing correctly?**
    - Yes → **Are your fonts and colours showing correctly?**
      - Yes → Go to D
      - No → Go to E
    - No → Go to A
- Yes → **Is it a '404' or a 'Page Not Found' Error?**
  - No → Go to B
  - Yes → **Are your Nameservers correct?**
    - Yes → Go to F
    - No → Go to C

Site Hit the Fan?...

A - Bad Links
Hover your mouse over a link. A the bottom of the browser you should be able to see where that link goes to. Does it look correct?

The most common error made by new website creators is linking to files on your own computer. A link should look like this: 'http://mywebsite.com/page.html'.

It should not look like this: 'C:\mywebsite\page.html' - if it does, you've made a link to your computer and not the page. In your code editor, remove everything from the link apart from the actual file name.

The same applies to images. If all else fails, try entering a direct link to the image on your hosting server. For example: http://mywebsite.com/images/image1.jpg

B - Error Page
A '404 - Page Not Found' means the page does not exist. However, if you have received a different error there is another problem. Any error that starts with the number 5 relates to a server error - you should contact your hosting provider for assistance.

There are alot of error codes used so it might be worth while checking the following page and then performing an internet search:

http://en.wikipedia.org/wiki/List_of_HTTP_status_codes

C - Wrong Name Servers
Head back to the page where we discussed name serves. You will need to get the correct nameservers from your hosting provider and update your domain. Remember, it takes upto 24 hours for this change to happen!

Site Hit the Fan?...

D - The Unknown
Based on your answers there is something wrong with your site that is not covered by this book. However, your basic site should be online. If you require further help try an internet search for your problem or contact a company such as NovusManagement.co.uk who specialise in helping sites manage themselves.

E - Fonts or Colours Not Showing Correct
If your fonts are not showing correctly go back to your Code Editor and double check you have entered the settings you want. If the problem still persists, go back to the page on fonts and check your using a standard font.

F - Nameservers Correct but Site Not Working
If your nameservers are correct but you still get a 404 Error you need to check that you have uploaded your website to the right folder. You will need to check with your hosting provider but it is normally 'www' or 'public'.

If your still having problems with your website try searching forums for answers - or even posting your problem. If your having a issue, chances are many people have experienced it too.

Sometimes, if you feel its all getting too complicated, you can try starting again from fresh - I find this is a good way to solve an issue when there is just too much to check.

Glossary...

The world of computers and web design is littered with silly sounding words and abbreviations. The glossary should help you decipher some of the words.

Bandwidth
Bandwidth is the amount of data you can transfer from your hosting server to your visitors computer. View the page about hosting for more information.

CSS
Cascading Style Sheets is a very useful way of maintaining the appearance of your website. It allows you to make groups of styles which can be applied to multiple parts of your website. This makes it easy to edit later and your website faster to load.

DHTML
Dynamic HTML is a mixture of different coding languages including CSS and JavaScript which allows you to add extra features to your site.

DNS
Domain Name Service - this is the name of the system that controls the relationship between computers and web address.

HTML
Hypertext Markup Language is the very basic code used to make even the simplest of websites. Think of it as the building-blocks of your site. You should learn HTML if you want to make a good website.

HTTP
Hypertext Transfer Protocol - this refers to a set of rules that control the connection and transfer of data between your computer and web servers. Secure connections are known as HTTPS (note the extra S for "Secure").

Glossary...

Hyperlink
A hyperlink is a link between two things on the internet. When you click on a link to move between pages you are clicking on a hyperlink.

IP
This stands for 'Internet Protocol'. Every computer is assigned a number which is known as its IP. Usually they consist of four sets of numbers seperated by a dot. For Example: 192.168.0.1

URL
This is the fancy word for the web address you type in to visit a website. The full name is 'Universal Resource Locator' - I think 'Web Address' is simpler...

W3C
You may come across this term on the internet when looking for help. The W3C is an organisation which helps provide a standard for website design (amongst other things). Their website has alot of useful information and tools you might be interested in.

WYSIWYG
Ironically, one of the simpliest terms in the geek world. It simply stands for 'What You See Is What You Get' and means that what you see in your Code Editor is what you will see online (in theory).

About The Author...

Carl Mason is a Freelance Website Designer based in the West Midlands (UK) and is a partner in C2Digital - an online company offering a variety of services including website design and management.

You can contact the author by emailing: carl.mason@c2publishing.co.uk

For more information, or to seek the help of Carl, you can visit either the C2Digital.co.uk website or the NovusDesigns.co.uk website.

Website Discount...

If, after reading this book, you have decided you would rather have your website designed and managed by a professional, you can take advantage of our 20% discount offer.

All you need to do is quote the discount code below when you speak to one of our designers:

X92K1JDD

Further Reading...

We hope you have enjoyed this book. It is the first of a series we hope to publish. You can find details of any new books by visiting out website: C2Publishing.co.uk.

Here is a list of books we are hoping to publish soon...

- [ ] Website Troubleshooter
- [ ] HTML Crash Course
- [ ] CSS Crash Course
- [ ] PHP Crash Course
- [ ] Website Marketing
- [ ] Search Engine Optimization
- [ ] How to Make a Website for £20

Printed in Great Britain
by Amazon.co.uk, Ltd.,
Marston Gate.